Bodies of Water

# Oceans and Seas

Cassie Mayer

Heinemann
LIBRARY

First published in Great Britain by Heinemann Library,
Halley Court, Jordan Hill, Oxford OX2 8EJ, part of Harcourt
Education. Heinemann is a registered trademark of Harcourt
Education Ltd.

© Harcourt Education Ltd 2007
The moral right of the proprietor has been asserted.

Editorial: Diyan Leake and Cassie Mayer
Design: Joanna Hinton-Malivoire
Picture research: Erica Martin
Production: Duncan Gilbert

Originated by Chroma Graphics (Overseas) Pte Ltd
Printed and bound in China by South China Printing Co. Ltd

ISBN 978 0 4311 8470 8

11 10 09 08 07
10 9 8 7 6 5 4 3 2 1

**British Library Cataloguing in Publication Data**
Mayer, Cassie
Bodies of Water: Oceans and Seas

A full catalogue record for this book is available from the
British Library

**Acknowledgements**
The publishers would like to thank the following for permission
to reproduce photographs: Alamy pp. **5** (eye35.com ),
**18** (Michael Diggin); Corbis pp. **4** (NASA), **10** (Blaine
Harrington III), **13** (Zefa/Gary Bell), **15** (Steve Terrill), **19**
(Zefa/Wilfried Krecichwost), **20** (Onne van der Wal), **23**
(barge: Onne van der Wal; kelp: Zefa/Gary Bell; beach:
Zefa/Wilfried Krecichwost), **back cover** (Zefa/Wilfried
Krecichwost); Getty Images p. **6** (Raphael Van Butsele);
**14**, **21** (Alison Langley); Jupiter Images pp. **7** (Dynamic
Graphics), **11**; Nature Picture Library p. **12** (Georgette
Douwma); Photolibrary pp. **16** (Sue Scott), **17** (Sue Scott).

Cover photograph of an ocean wave reproduced with
permission of Corbis/Zefa (Jason Hosking).

Every effort has been made to contact copyright holders
of any material reproduced in this book. Any omissions will
be rectified in subsequent printings if notice is given to the
publishers.

# Contents

# Oceans

water

Most of the Earth is covered by water.

Most of this water is in oceans.

An ocean is a large area covered by water.

Oceans have salty water.

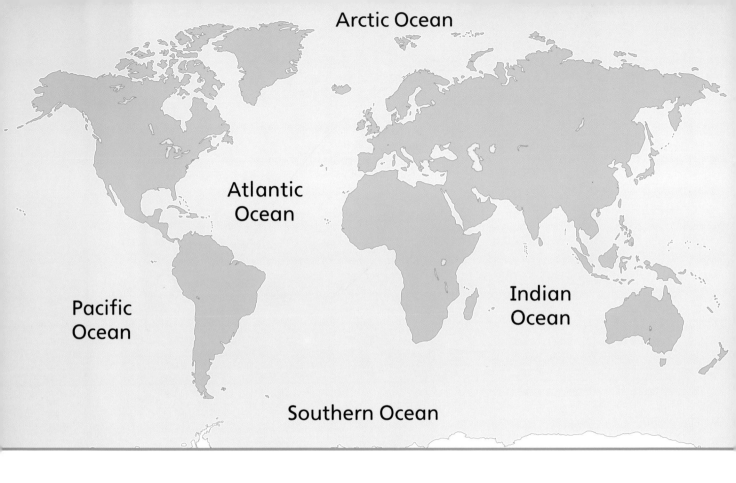

There are five oceans.

North America

Europe

Asia

Africa

South America

Australia

continent

There is land in between the oceans.
Each big piece of land is a continent.

# Seas

sea

Most seas are smaller parts of oceans.

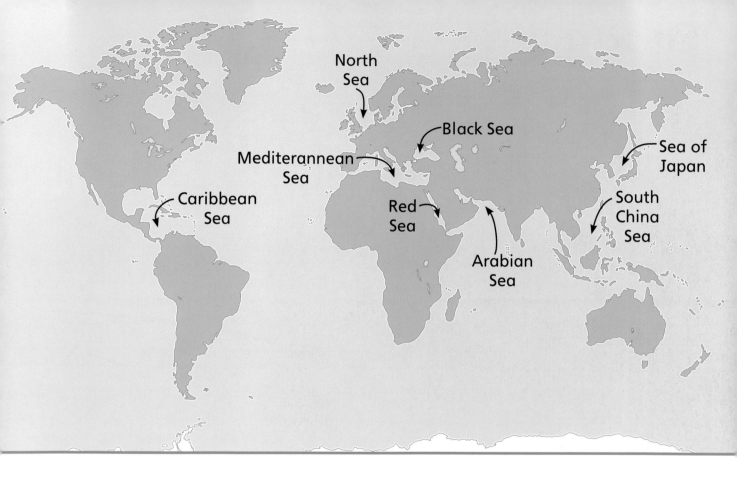

North Sea

Black Sea

Sea of Japan

Mediterannean Sea

Caribbean Sea

Red Sea

South China Sea

Arabian Sea

There are many seas.

# Ocean life

There are many animals in the ocean.

seaweed

There are many plants in the ocean.

# Ocean movements

Wind moves across oceans.

The wind makes waves.

Waves wear away the rocks on the coasts.

Ocean water rises on to the beaches.
We say this is when the tide is in.

The ocean waters fall back again.
We say this is when the tide is out.

When the tide is in, the water is deep.
It covers the beaches and some rocks.

When the tide is out, we can see
more of the beach.

# How we use oceans

Big ships take goods across the oceans to different places.

Some people like to sail across
the oceans.

# Ocean facts

The Pacific Ocean is the largest ocean in the world.

The Mariana Trench is the deepest part of the ocean. It is in the Pacific Ocean.

# Picture glossary

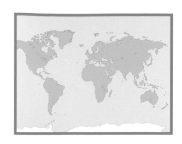 **continent** a large piece of land

 **goods** things that people buy and sell

 **tide** a change in ocean water level

 **seaweed** a plant in the ocean

# Index

**Note to Parents and Teachers**

**Before reading**

Ask the children if they have ever been to the seaside. What did they see? Did they see how water sometimes come right in to the land and sometimes goes away from the land? Do they know what this is called? (Tides) Explain that the sea is part of an ocean. There are five oceans in the world.

**After reading**

*Clapping game.* Teach the children the rhyme "A sailor went to sea, sea, sea / To see what he could see, see, see / But all that he could see, see, see / Was the bottom of the deep blue sea, sea, sea." Tell the children to work out a clapping sequence with a partner and to sing the song as they clap.

*Ocean story.* Read the book *The Rainbow Fish* or another Rainbow Fish story

*Fish hand prints.* Make hand prints on scraps of coloured card and cut out them. Turn the hand print sideways and draw an eye and a mouth. Suspend the fish from the ceiling or make a collage of the fish.

Fish. Show the children a live fish in a fish tank. Ask them to notice how it swims. What does it do with its mouth? What does it do with its tail and fins?